NICHOLAS WRIGHT

Nicholas Wright's plays include *Vincent in Brixton* (Olivier Award for Best New Play, 2003) and the original production of *Mrs Klein*, both at the National Theatre, in the West End and in New York; *Treetops* and *One Fine Day* at Riverside Studios; *The Gorky Brigade* at the Royal Court; *The Crimes of Vautrin* for Joint Stock; *The Custom of the Country* and *The Desert Air* for the RSC; *Cressida* for the Almeida and *The Reporter* at the National. Adaptations include *His Dark Materials*, *Three Sisters* and *John Gabriel Borkman* for the National; *Thérèse Raquin* at Chichester Festival Theatre and the National; and *Naked* and *Lulu* at the Almeida. He wrote the libretti for Rachel Portman's opera *The Little Prince* (Houston Grand Opera) and for Jonathan Dove's opera for television, *Man on the Moon*, based on the Apollo 11 moon landing. Other writing for television includes adaptations of *More Tales of the City* and *The No. 1 Ladies' Detective Agency* (BBC/HBO). His writing about the theatre includes *99 Plays*, a personal view of playwriting from Aeschylus to the present day, and *Changing Stages: A View of British Theatre in the Twentieth Century*, co-written with Richard Eyre.

Nicholas Wright

MRS KLEIN

NICK HERN BOOKS
London
www.nickhernbooks.co.uk

A Nick Hern Book

Mrs Klein first published in 1988 by Nick Hern Books Limited, 14 Larden Road, London W3 7ST

This revised edition published in 2009

Mrs Klein copyright © 1988, 2009 Nicholas Wright

Nicholas Wright has asserted his right to be identified as the author of this work

Nicholas Wright gratefully acknowledges the use of Phyllis Grosskurth's biography *Melanie Klein*, published by Hodder and Stoughton, 1985

Front cover: George Marks/Retrofile RF/Getty Images
Cover design: Ned Hoste, 2H

Typeset by Nick Hern Books, London
Printed in the UK by CPI Antony Rowe, Chippenham, Wiltshire

A CIP catalogue record for this book is available from the British Library

ISBN 978 1 84842 066 3

FSC
Mixed Sources
Product group from well-managed
forests and other controlled sources
Cert no. SGS-COC-2953
www.fsc.org
© 1996 Forest Stewardship Council

Mrs Klein was first performed in the Cottesloe auditorium of the National Theatre, London, on 10 August 1988 (previews from 5 August), with the following cast:

MRS KLEIN   Gillian Barge
PAULA   Zoë Wanamaker
MELITTA   Francesca Annis

Director   Peter Gill
Designer   John Gunter
Costume Designer   Stephen Brimson-Lewis
Composer   Terry Davies

This production transferred to London's West End at the end of 1988.

The play was first staged on Broadway in Autumn 1995, directed by William Carden, with Uta Hagen as Mrs Klein. The play has also been staged in Berlin, France, Australia, New Zealand, Johannesburg, Washington DC and Copenhagen.

Mrs Klein was revived at the Almeida Theatre, London, on 29 October 2009 (previews from 22 October), with the following cast:

MRS KLEIN   Clare Higgins
PAULA   Nicola Walker
MELITTA   Zoë Waites

Director   Thea Sharrock
Designer   Tim Hatley
Lighting Designer   Neil Austin
Sound Designer   Ian Dickinson for Autograph

Characters

MRS KLEIN, *fifty-two*

PAULA, *early thirties*

MELITTA, *early thirties*

Place

London

Time

Spring 1934

Note on the Text

A forward slash (/) in the text indicates the point at which the next speaker interrupts.

ACT ONE

MRS KLEIN *is sorting through old papers.* PAULA *is listening.*

MRS KLEIN. It's quite incredible what one keeps.

Tears up a photograph. Finds a piece of paper.

This is a poem he wrote.

Reads it.

Excuse me.

She cries. Holds her hand out. PAULA *takes it.* MRS KLEIN *slowly stops crying.*

I think that's it till next time. So: our coffee should be ready. You'll have some?

PAULA. Thank you.

MRS KLEIN. Now, what's this?

PAULA. I've brought you something.

It's a cake box.

MRS KLEIN. But, my dear, you shouldn't have spent your money. No, don't tell me.

Opens it.

Paula, this is most intuitive of you. Poppy-seed cake, no reason you should know this, was my mother's speciality.

Gives PAULA *the poem.*

You can read this.

She goes out. PAULA *reads.* MRS KLEIN *comes back with coffee. Pours.*

I'm in a very adequate state, all things considered. I cough a lot but then I'm smoking more. I sleep enough, not much. I have my knock-out drops if I should need them but I'm holding off so far. No dreams, which is unusual for me. Normally I'm an active, colourful dreamer. Now, each night, the show is cancelled. Most annoying. Milk?

PAULA. Thank you.

MRS KLEIN. You're welcome. Chiefly what I feel is numbness. Here inside. As though some vital part of me had been removed. The tears don't help. All they do is make a thorough nuisance of themselves. And then they stop and leave me feeling exactly as I did before. Remote. Closed up. And dead. You'll have some cake?

PAULA. Yes, thank you.

MRS KLEIN. So: my work goes on. I read, I write, I entertain a few old friends, I see my patients. Clear a space. I'm on my own today. My cleaning woman has a family crisis in Southend. Or so she says. The truth is that she needs a break from my unnatural calm. And so do I. But there we are, I may not like it but I'm stuck with it. I don't know why. I don't have insight into my emotions, not just now. Some other time. So: eat.

They do.

But why no dreams? No, that's enough about me. The poem, you read it?

PAULA. Yes.

MRS KLEIN. So tell me.

PAULA. It was written when he was young.

MRS KLEIN. He was. He was a boy, he was fifteen.

PAULA. It's a love poem. Though the woman seems older than him. Who was she?

MRS KLEIN. I doubt she ever existed. Not in life. Though, to my son, of course, she breathed, she moved, she comforted. She was the mother.

PAULA. Yes, I see.

MRS KLEIN. She was myself.

She takes back the poem.

I'm very grateful that you could come at such short notice. I would like you to do some work for me while I'm away.

PAULA. What kind of work?

MRS KLEIN. You're not too busy?

PAULA. No.

MRS KLEIN. Thank God, thank God! Have some more cake.

PAULA. No, thank you.

MRS KLEIN *has some more.*

MRS KLEIN. I'm famished. I've been eating scraps. Cheese on toast, sardines on toast, ridiculous. And so this morning I got up and cooked myself a hearty British breakfast. Then I looked at it. Then I gave it to the Pekinese.

PAULA *looks round for it.*

He's not here now. He'll be living the life of Riley for the next ten days, in kennels, up by Primrose Hill. He won't be bothering you. His name is Nanki-Poo. A wandering minstrel, he. You know your Gilbert and Sullivan?

PAULA. When you say he won't be bothering me – ?

MRS KLEIN. Quite so. Let me explain.

A set of keys.

These are my spare keys to the front door. My cleaning woman has her own. Keys to the rooms upstairs, my bedroom, my consulting room, I'm putting somewhere safe. She'll tell you if you ask, but for emergencies. She says she'll water the plants. If you could watch the window boxes. Let me see.

Her notebook.

PAULA. I'm sorry. Do you want me to / look after the house?

MRS KLEIN. There's more to come. I made a list. I felt compelled to. And this in itself is strange, because my memory's good. I woke at four o'clock this morning, wondering, 'What am I making lists for, is there perhaps some paranoiac aspect to it?' but I couldn't think it through at that hour. I've stopped the milk. I've stopped *The Times*, I've stopped the *Daily Mail*. The central heating has instructions pinned above it. Sunny is with my daughter. Sunny is the car, the Sunbeam. Make of it what you will. Food is in the fridge, and when you leave at night, please check the windows and, of course, the door. Now, is there anything else domestic? Good.

PAULA. When you say, 'leave at night', / do you mean that...?

MRS KLEIN. If I could do my list? And questions after.

At the desk.

Letters here. Periodicals here. Messages on this pad.

Letters.

These I would appreciate your posting for me.

A pin box.

I've left some money here for odd expenses and your travel. I won't feel happy otherwise. I'll worry that you're feeling in some way imposed upon. So spend it freely. Here. Five shillings. Good, that's settled.

Another letter.

This, I don't know what to do with. It arrived this morning. Marked, 'To await return'. It comes from Dr Schmideberg. I don't like it. I don't even like the envelope. It looks as though it's about to burst with hostile matter. This is what professional enemies are like. They're vampires. They're dependent. They want love. And so they nag and pester. Should I read it? Should I throw it away? If I throw it away, can I blame the post? I'll... No, I can't decide.

She puts it down.

At such a time I don't deserve to be so persecuted. Next. The proofs.

PAULA. The proofs?

MRS KLEIN. You know the system?

PAULA. If you tell me what it is that you / want, I'll do what
    I…

MRS KLEIN. Fine, come look.

Proofs on the desk.

You've read the book?

PAULA. Of course, I –

MRS KLEIN. I knew you would have. This will be the second
    German-language edition.

A book.

This is the first. There are some misprints which I've put a
ring round. So you must check both. I've marked in pencil
where I want revisions.

Notes.

These are they. This arrow goes back, then skip, then on,
yes?

Another book.

Some revisions, though not all, are in the second English
edition, here.

A dictionary.

English-German, German-English.

Manuscript.

Here's the new chapter. So you must watch the numbering.

Another manuscript.

This is the foreword. Do you type?

PAULA. Two fingers.

MRS KLEIN. Likewise. Three copies. Carbon here. You
    understand?

PAULA. Yes.

MRS KLEIN. Sure?

PAULA. Quite sure. When is the copy date?

MRS KLEIN. Forget the copy date, it's weeks ago, I want them posted to Vienna first post Wednesday at the latest.

PAULA. Fine. I'll show you what I've done on Tuesday.

MRS KLEIN. But I won't be here on Tuesday.

PAULA. You won't – ?

MRS KLEIN. I have a funeral to attend.

PAULA. I'm sorry, yes, of course. So will you –

MRS KLEIN. I shall be back from Budapest the following weekend.

PAULA. Then you won't have seen them.

MRS KLEIN. Plainly not.

PAULA. So if there's anything I get wrong –

MRS KLEIN. They'll print it wrong and I'll look stupid. But I'm not expecting that to happen.

PAULA. Why?

MRS KLEIN. Because I trust you.

PAULA. But we've never really met. You hardly know me.

MRS KLEIN. I've seen you often at the Institute, you're highly thought of. Will you do it?

PAULA. Yes.

MRS KLEIN. You're a good girl. I didn't ask if you'd like a glass of sherry.

She goes to get it.

PAULA. No.

MRS KLEIN. Too early? Likewise.

She comes back. Pause. Relaxed. They are both accustomed to long pauses.

Besides, I liked your comments after Edward Glover gave his verdict on my criminality paper. At that Scientific Meeting. You were very acute. You shut him up for weeks, that's no mean feat. Tell me, which of the two, in your opinion, has sown more discord in the world of psycho-analysis? Glover or Schmideberg? No, I mustn't compromise you. Glover's not a dunce exactly but he's too dogmatic. Dr Schmideberg needs help.

Pause.

The heck with it.

She goes to the drinks cabinet and pours two sherries.

So we've never met? I felt I knew you.

PAULA. We've been introduced. But we've never / spent any time together…

MRS KLEIN. Never sat and talked. It's very pleasant. And I'm glad you arrived a fraction late. I was with a patient. Nine years old last week. So, not my youngest but my most demanding. He wouldn't stay in the consulting room today, he felt it pressing in on him, he took against it. So we came down here. There, that's his train, his 'Daddy-train' he calls it. He played, I played. If you'd rung the bell I wouldn't have let you in. Because my patients cannot be disturbed. The world must wait. I'm sure you feel the same. Now, this is a Manzanilla which I'm rather proud of.

They sit and drink their sherry. Pause.

MRS KLEIN. You've been in London now…?

PAULA. Six months.

MRS KLEIN. You have family in Berlin?

PAULA. I do.

MRS KLEIN. You hear from them?

PAULA. My mother writes. My brothers.

MRS KLEIN. Have you sisters?

PAULA. No.

MRS KLEIN. That's not a simple 'no'.

PAULA. I had an older sister.

MRS KLEIN. Were you close in age?

PAULA. She died before I was born.

MRS KLEIN. So you're important to your mother.

PAULA. Yes.

MRS KLEIN. To comfort her. Or so you see it. And you're married?

PAULA. Yes.

MRS KLEIN. He's not an analyst?

PAULA. He's a doctor.

MRS KLEIN. That isn't what I asked.

PAULA. He's not an analyst.

MRS KLEIN. He doesn't approve?

PAULA. He doesn't approve.

MRS KLEIN. And where've you put him?

PAULA. Where – ?

MRS KLEIN. He's not in England?

PAULA. No. In Zurich.

MRS KLEIN. Ah. So did he – ?

PAULA. He left Germany first. Because he had to. I stayed on. Because there wasn't so much pressure on me.

MRS KLEIN. Though I heard you'd been arrested.

PAULA. It wasn't serious. They searched the house and took some books and they finally dropped the charges.

MRS KLEIN. It frightened you.

PAULA. Yes.

MRS KLEIN. You're Jewish.

PAULA. Yes. But it was worse for him. My husband. He was
more political than I am.

MRS KLEIN. When you say your husband *was* political, do
you mean he isn't now or that he's no longer your husband?

PAULA. We're divorced.

MRS KLEIN. And how do you find it?

PAULA. Lonely.

MRS KLEIN. Likewise.

Gives PAULA *her glass, marks a place on it with her
fingers.*

I can manage that much more. And help yourself.

PAULA *pours sherry.*

My son was involved in politics when he was younger. Just
like in any intellectual family. But I've never been political
myself. Although I've had good cause to be. I've been spat at
in the street. My children too. And now I hear each week
from friends at home, they've had their windows smashed,
the Star of David painted on the doors, the papers scattered,
the children in tears. I know about it, thank you, and it won't
get better. I can't stop it. You can't. Can your husband? In
these terrible times we live in? And it doesn't interest me to
try. That's not my calling.

She sees her sherry, drinks.

Somebody said you had a daughter.

PAULA. What?

MRS KLEIN. Your daughter.

PAULA. I've a daughter, yes. She's nine years old. She's in
Berlin. She's with some Catholic friends.

MRS KLEIN. And will she join you?

PAULA. I hope so. Soon. Only…

MRS KLEIN. So what is your problem?

PAULA. I'll need a decent place to live.

MRS KLEIN. Where are you now?

PAULA. In Bethnal Green.

MRS KLEIN. I've never been there. What's it like?

PAULA. It's horrible. It's a slum.

MRS KLEIN. Do you practise there?

PAULA. I try to.

MRS KLEIN. It must be hard.

PAULA. It's impossible. Either my patients can't afford to pay me or they leave.

MRS KLEIN. It's early days.

PAULA. I'm thirty-four. I don't have a proper coat. I've never lived like this.

MRS KLEIN. You're angry.

PAULA. Yes.

MRS KLEIN. You should apply to change your visa. Then you can practise in whatever part of London appeals to you.

PAULA. I've applied already. They turned me down.

MRS KLEIN. Apply again. I'll put a word in for you this time. No, don't thank me, I do little enough for new arrivals. Pass me that box.

It's the box with Hans's letters in it.

I feel that Hans would like his poem to go to you.

She gives PAULA *the scrap of paper.*

PAULA. I can't accept it.

MRS KLEIN. No strings. Take it.

PAULA. Thank you.

She takes it.

MRS KLEIN. But there's something on your mind.

PAULA. I don't know why you're doing this. I don't know why
you're letting me help you. Isn't there somebody else who
you could ask?

MRS KLEIN. I can't imagine who you mean.

PAULA. You have your English friends.

MRS KLEIN. I was holidaying in St Ives last week and a very
good English friend came with me. Mrs Rivière. I like her,
she's a loyal colleague and an adequate clinician, not out-
standing. We stayed a week, then motored back and stopped
in Salisbury. A bed-and-breakfast place, no heating, didn't
like dogs and Mrs Rivière discovered that she'd left her fox
fur back in Cornwall. This is a woman who takes a fox fur
on a walking holiday. So she rang the hotel, and suddenly it's
the manager's wife on the telephone. 'Is that Mrs Klein?'
'No, it's her friend, I think I left my fox fur on the terrace – '
But it's me the woman wants to talk to. There's been a telephone call from Budapest, a foreign lady, Mrs Vago. 'Yes,' I
say. 'My sister-in-law.' And what was so important that she
telephones? I'd left the number here, so – 'Is it bad news?' I
ask. The woman says: 'It is my duty – ' She was trying to be
considerate. I say, 'Don't go around the houses, I'm a grown-
up woman, I'm sitting down.' She says, 'It's about your son.
He's had a climbing accident.' I'm sitting in the hallway
looking at a green baize board with postcards on it. Stone-
henge. I was looking at it, thinking, 'What does that mean?'
She was talking. 'Are you there?' She thought I'd fainted. I
said: 'Tell me, please: this accident my son had: was it fatal?'
She replied: 'I'm sorry, Mrs Klein, you won't believe this
but I can't remember.' I said, 'Don't worry, I believe you, but
I can't explain it to you, not right now, just tell me: have you
written it down?' She says: 'I'll find it.' I waited. In a state of
some suspense. I heard her shuffling papers, banging
drawers. Then it struck me: how, without appearing callous,
would I raise the subject of Mrs Rivière's fox fur? And I was

worried about her fur because I didn't *really*, *absolutely* think she'd sympathise. Although she did. And she was admirable. But yet I didn't trust her. Why? Because I don't trust any English people. Not with this. Not now. They don't feel home-like. I want my home around me. I want the good things close and safe. I want to hear the German language. You speak German and you bring me poppy-seed cake. Also, I like you.

She passes the box to PAULA.

Put it beneath the stairs and bring my coat and hat. And my umbrella. And my bags, no, leave them there but count them, there are two and a hatbox.

PAULA. Are you leaving now?

MRS KLEIN. Yes, now, the taxi's due in – Check the gloves are in the pockets.

PAULA *gets her coat, etc., while* MRS KLEIN *writes down a telephone number.* PAULA *comes back with coat, etc.*

You can reach me at this number. Budapest is not that far, my sister-in-law speaks perfect German. As you see, I wish to reassure you that I haven't died. Now, do I need to spend a penny. No.

She dresses.

I won't suggest you see me to the station. You'd be better advised to start the work at once.

Checks in her notebook.

Scissors. Needles. Who needs needles?

Doorbell rings.

Ticket. Passport. Money. Glasses.

Doorbell.

Glasses. Glasses. Say I'm ready. Take the bags out.

PAULA *goes out.* MRS KLEIN *finds her glasses.*

Keys.

*She takes a large bunch of keys out of her handbag. Locks
the drinks cabinet. Finds Dr Schmideberg's letter and puts it
in the filing cabinet. At some point the taxi driver toots his
horn.* MRS KLEIN *makes a space in the bookshelf, puts the
keys in the space, selects a book and puts it back on the shelf
where it conceals the keys. One last look round. She goes
out.*

PAULA *comes back. Puts on a light, draws the curtains. Sits
at the desk, moves things round to find a working order.
Starts work.*

Music.

Time passes.

Some hours later. PAULA *is still working. Front door heard
opening and closing.*

PAULA. Hello?

MELITTA *comes in.*

MELITTA. What the bloody hell are you doing here?

PAULA. I'm reading proofs.

MELITTA. What for?

PAULA. She asked me to.

MELITTA. When?

PAULA. This afternoon.

MELITTA. She wasn't here this afternoon.

PAULA. Yes, she was. I saw her.

MELITTA. Here?

PAULA. Yes, here.

MELITTA. Oh, Jesus Christ.

PAULA. What is it?

MELITTA. Nothing.

PAULA. Would you like some coffee?

MELITTA. No. I need a drink. And you?

PAULA. I'm not thirsty.

MELITTA. Never stopped *me*.

Tries the drinks cupboard.

It's locked.

PAULA. Let me try it.

Does.

That's strange.

Tries again.

It is. I'm sorry.

MELITTA. Darling, it's not your fault. You carry on.

PAULA. I will. Did that sound rude? She wants them done by Wednesday and it's taken me four hours to do one chapter.

Pause. MELITTA *moves around the room.*

MELITTA. Aren't you freezing?

PAULA. No.

MELITTA. Why don't you go and put the heating on?

PAULA. I tried. It didn't light and I was worried I might break it so I left it. Let me finish.

Pause. MELITTA *looks over* PAULA's *shoulder at her work.*

MELITTA. I'm in this.

PAULA. I know, I've just been doing the footnote.

MELITTA. And that's not an ashtray.

PAULA. No?

MELITTA. It's part of a coffee set.

Replaces saucer with ashtray.

Here.

Empties stubs, moves around, stacks sherry glasses and
generally tidies up.

PAULA. Are you here for something special?

MELITTA. No, I happened to be driving past and saw the light
on. Someone's moved a book.

PAULA. Not me.

MELITTA. So let me get this straight, you saw her here this
afternoon.

PAULA. That's right.

MELITTA. Because she should have left on Tuesday.

PAULA. No, she left as planned. I'm sure of that. Because
when Walter rang me –

MELITTA. *Walter* rang you?

PAULA. Yes, he –

MELITTA. Why?

PAULA. He had a message. He said she wanted me to call on
her. She'd got my letter, and she…

MELITTA. Letter?

PAULA. Yes. I wrote a letter of condolence. Everyone else was
writing to her. I assumed you wouldn't mind.

MELITTA. Why should I mind?

PAULA. I mean, I didn't think *she'd* mind.

MELITTA. And so the sequence was: you wrote a letter to my
mother and she sent an invitation via my husband. That's
what happened.

PAULA. That's what happened.

MELITTA. And?

PAULA. She asked me to look after the / house while…

MELITTA. No, not you.

PAULA. Your mother?

MELITTA. Yes, my mother. How did she seem?

PAULA tidies her papers for an orderly start next day.

PAULA. Her dreams have stopped, I don't know if she told you. And she cries from time to time but the tears don't help. She's still denying the loss. Is this what you want to know, I don't – ?

MELITTA. Go on.

PAULA. She's trying to reinstate the lost loved object: keeping Hans's letters in a place of safety. Tearing other papers up, because she sees them perhaps as hostile. She has periods of elation. She's not eating properly. She's in mourning.

MELITTA. Did she mention me?

PAULA. She said you had the car.

MELITTA. What else?

PAULA. I don't remember.

MELITTA. You're a liar.

PAULA. That may be. I can't discuss it, not at this time of night. I'm sorry, Melitta.

She goes out. MELITTA *tries to open the top drawer of the filing cabinet. Locked. Goes to desk, rummages round in top drawers. Finds only pins, elastic bands, etc. Moves away.* PAULA *comes back wearing a coat and hat.*

MELITTA. You've got your coat on.

PAULA. Yes. It's late, I'll miss my Underground.

MELITTA. I'll drive you home.

PAULA. What for?

MELITTA. Oh, don't you want me to?

PAULA. I'd love you to. I hate the Tube. It's full of drunks and madmen. But it just so happens that through no decision of my own I live the other end of London.

MELITTA. But I've got the car.

PAULA. I'll pay for the petrol.

MELITTA. Rubbish, you can't afford it.

PAULA. Fine. Let's go.

MELITTA. Let's stay for a moment.

PAULA. Not too long. I'm tired. (*Her eyes are strained.*) I have to check each word. Although she's changing nothing essential. Misprints. Extra footnotes. Foreword. Brand-new chapter. (*Laughs.*) Quite a lot, in fact, but nothing essential.

MELITTA. So you're doing her secretarial work?

PAULA. Not really.

MELITTA. And her letters, will you file her letters?

PAULA. No.

MELITTA. Although they're streaming in in sackfuls, so it seems.

PAULA. They won't need filing.

MELITTA. So you'll put them where?

PAULA. In here. (*Basket.*) The filing cabinet's locked.

MELITTA. That's a bore. She asked me to collect some papers. But I don't know where the keys are.

PAULA. I don't know.

MELITTA. Well, somebody must.

PAULA. The cleaning woman knows. They had an arrangement, hide them – somewhere in the house, I don't know where, it's not my business.

Pause.

Most of the house is locked. She's locked the cellar door, she's locked the rooms upstairs. It's symbolic. The house is her.

PAULA *smiles.*

Let's go.

MELITTA. When I was briefly – fairly briefly – couple of months – or less – prevailed upon to be her private secretary – I threw a vase and hit that bit of wall behind your head.

PAULA. I'm reading proofs. Which suits me fine. I don't like weekends at the best of times, they're lonely and depressing so I don't mind helping. But I'm not her secretary. I'm not her anything else, let's make that clear.

MELITTA *looks up a number in her address book.*

MELITTA. There's a fascinating paper by Ferenczi on neurotic weekends. He says that during the week our work routine soaks up aggressive feelings.

Finds number. Dials.

But then at weekends they let fly. That's why Sunday's the day we dread the most. It's a Pandora's box stuffed full of nameless hatreds. And the lid not properly closed. (*To telephone.*) Oh, bloody answer. Stupid savages. Hello. Oh, thank you, can I speak to Mrs P? (*To herself.*) Oh, bugger. Pow. Pownall. (*To telephone.*) Mrs Pountney. Phew. Yes, this is Dr Schmideberg speaking. S-C-H – Doctor, that's right. No, no one's ill, I simply – (*To* PAULA *in comic cockney.*) 'Gawn to fetch 'er 'usband.' (*To telephone.*) Hello. This is – No, there's nothing wrong. I have your name down here in my address book as an avenue to Mrs Pountney, I believe she lives on the floor above you. Yes, I do, it's twenty to eleven.

PAULA. Melitta.

MELITTA, *in fury, bangs the telephone on the desk.*

MELITTA. I'm sorry, I dropped the phone. That's very kind, if you could see if she's there. Tell her it's Melitta. She knows me, yes, she very kindly cleans my mother's house for her. Tell her I'm there, I'm here, and everything's locked up and ask her where the keys are. No, there isn't any need to – (*To* PAULA.) Now he's putting his wife back on.

PAULA. Melitta.

MELITTA. What?

PAULA. She's gone away for the weekend.

MELITTA. Mrs Pountney?

PAULA *nods*.

(*To telephone*.) One moment, please. (*To* PAULA.) Has she gone far?

PAULA. To South – South something.

MELITTA. Southport? Southsea?

PAULA. No, it's something anal.

MELITTA. Southend.

PAULA. That sounds right.

MELITTA (*to telephone*). Thank you, I've just found out. Goodnight.

Rings off.

Damn that woman. Damn her. God rot her to hell. Vile crone. I've begged my mother a thousand times to sack her. But she won't. She can't. She sees the cleaning woman as her mother. Wouldn't you say?

PAULA. I've no idea, Melitta. Can we go now?

MELITTA. Did she get my letter?

PAULA. Yes.

MELITTA. Did she read it?

PAULA. Not while I was there. She said you'd marked it 'To await return'. No, let's be frank. She felt attacked by it. So she was hostile to the letter and to you. But not to you, her daughter. No. To Dr Schmideberg. She only referred to you as Dr Schmideberg. The daughter's good, she loves her, but the doctor's bad, it's casebook stuff. It won't last. She'll read your letter soon. In fact she probably took it with her.

MELITTA. Jesus Christ.

PAULA. What now?

MELITTA. I'm feeling sick.

PAULA. Do you want a glass of water?

MELITTA. No.

PAULA. Try putting your head between your knees.

MELITTA. I need a drink.

PAULA. Let's see what we can do.

Goes to the drinks cabinet. Examines it. Takes out the top drawer.

I thought so.

Reaches down inside.

One can always find a way in somehow, as my professor would say.

Gets bottle and glasses out.

Whiskey? There's two kinds. Oh, this is Irish. Irish-Scotch, that's rather amusing.

MELITTA. Pour it.

PAULA. Yes, I am doing.

MELITTA. One for you.

PAULA. I have.

They drink.

I bought a whiskey once in a public house in Bethnal Green. But it was such a noisy and disgusting place I couldn't enjoy it. This is different. This is home-like.

Pause.

MELITTA. Do you have those dreams where something absolutely vital has been hidden away? In some familiar place? You search and search. But the handles keep on coming off the doors. Or empty rooms are suddenly crowded. Or the railway ticket's missing from your handbag, or the platform's vanished. And you can't admit whatever it is you're doing. Because it's shameful. Do you?

PAULA. Not the same but – Yes.

MELITTA. It's not just me then.

PAULA. They're anxiety dreams. Everyone has them.

MELITTA. I feel I'm in one all the time.

PAULA. I dream I've killed a child. I told my analyst. She
interpreted that I'd felt deserted by her over the Easter break.
I said, 'It can't be that, I've been having this dream for thirty
years.' She said, 'Ah-ha, and my consulting room is number
30.'

MELITTA. Do our patients talk about us like that?

PAULA. Of course they do. How's your analyst?

MELITTA. She wasn't giving satisfaction so I sacked her.

PAULA. What went wrong?

MELITTA. I thought she was my mother. And I couldn't work
through it. I couldn't stop thinking, 'Damn the bitch,' or
'Does she love me?' So she thought, and I agreed, that I was
stuck in the transference. And on we slogged. For years and
years. And nothing changed. Except that, bit by bit, I realised
that to all intents and purposes she *was* my mother. It was
my mother put me on to her. She reads my mother's books,
she quotes them word for word and once a month she meets
her for tea at Whiteleys. And I couldn't bear it, darling.

PAULA. Who've you gone to?

MELITTA. Never you mind.

PAULA. I'd like to change my analyst.

MELITTA. Who do you have your eye on?

PAULA. Well, I know who I want, but I haven't dared ask her
yet.

MELITTA *stares at her. Then marks a level on the glass with
one finger.*

MELITTA. Be a good girl and fill it up to here this time.

PAULA *does. She looks at the bottle.*

PAULA. It's seven years old. She must be quite a connoisseur.

MELITTA. Oh, she is. We drove through France two years ago and, just as we were getting on quite well, she went in for a claret-tasting competition and won first prize. They'd never had a woman champion. Now the Mayor sends her a post-card every Christmas. She's a local hero.

PAULA *smiles*.

It isn't funny, being her daughter. Try it. Perhaps you have.

PAULA. I don't know what you mean.

MELITTA. You've changed.

PAULA. How's that?

MELITTA. You're like some stubborn, slow amoeba making its gains by stealth.

PAULA *goes to the pin box and rummages for her five shillings*.

Just what do you think you're doing?

PAULA. I'm getting a taxi.

MELITTA. Put that back.

PAULA. It's my expenses.

MELITTA. Well, you might have told me you had taxi money.

PAULA. I forgot.

MELITTA. Forgot. You didn't want to leave. You're burrowing in.

PAULA *throws the box on the ground. It opens and the money falls out*.

PAULA. I have a mother of my own. I don't need yours. If that's the undercurrent. Why do you think I'd want to hurt you? Why? You're like a sister to me. You've been kind and good and generous to me. Nobody else from home has helped me. Not till now. Until your mother, true. Who seems neurotically attached to me for some strange reason. Or some obvious reason. I can't help it. And I don't care tuppence for your boring little Oedipal tangles. I have other problems. I've a daughter in Berlin, I have consulting rooms in Bethnal Green.

MELITTA. Who put you there?

PAULA. Not her.

MELITTA. They all did. At the Institute. Refugees not wanted. Not in Hampstead. Too much healthy competition. That's why they've dumped you all in these extraordinary places. And she's right behind it.

PAULA. You don't surprise me. Analysts are only human. If you threaten our professional livelihoods you'll get some very primitive responses. That was grubby of you.

MELITTA. Did she tell you how Hans died?

PAULA. She said a climbing accident.

MELITTA. He killed himself.

Pause.

PAULA. How do you know?

MELITTA. I rang my aunt in Budapest. Auntie Jolan. Mrs Vago. Talks for ever, cost a fortune.

PAULA. And?

MELITTA. I could tell at once that she was hiding something. So I asked her very obliquely. Where Hans had been that morning. What he was wearing. All the little details that I needed to complete the picture. She didn't want to tell me. Started howling. Banged the phone down. But I'd got my answers. I've got good material and I've worked it through. I've reached the only possible interpretation.

PAULA. Did he leave a note?

MELITTA. No note. That's what he was like. He used to disappear for hours. She'd shake him. 'Where've you been? I thought the cart had run you over!' He'd say: 'I've not been anywhere, Mother.' Never let on. So he'd hardly leave her a suicide note. He wouldn't want to give her the satisfaction.

PAULA. Does she know?

MELITTA. Well, that depends on whether or not she read my letter.

PAULA. Oh, Melitta. She'll be devastated.

MELITTA. Yes, she will.

PAULA. You told her?

MELITTA. Yes!

PAULA. That's horrible.

MELITTA. Yes, I know.

PAULA. How could you?

MELITTA. Well, I think I must be barmy.

Another drink for both.

When you saw it, where was it left exactly?

PAULA. There. (*The desk.*) It's gone now.

MELITTA. Yes, I looked.

Pause.

PAULA. I'm starving.

MELITTA. Likewise.

Pause.

PAULA. Was it an angry letter?

MELITTA. It was very detailed. Very convincing. Very persecutorily sadistic.

PAULA. Oh my God.

MELITTA. Exactly.

Pause.

I was sitting in the Wigmore Hall tonight. And they were playing Schubert. So divine. And all that horrible hatred seeped away. I felt that I was looking at it from high up. From somewhere in the ceiling. It was like a pile of rotting clothes. I felt utterly sane. So I came round here to get my letter back. It seemed so simple. Now all I can imagine is my mother in her first-class Pullman, looking for some further reading, putting down her copy of the *Psychoanalytic Quarterly*...

She laughs.

PAULA. No, Melitta.

MELITTA. Or maybe her *Country Life*...

PAULA. Or *Vogue*!

They both giggle.

MELITTA. And she climbs into bed...

PAULA. No, berth!

MELITTA. What?

PAULA. Berth, you know the...

She gestures.

MELITTA. Berth, that's right, she takes her corsets off...

They both giggle furiously.

...then up she climbs and...

PAULA. ...and does her nightie up to her chin...

Both collapse with laughter.

MELITTA. And then she reads – she reads –

PAULA. 'You cow, you murderess – '

MELITTA. No no no – it's worse than that –

PAULA. 'You bitch, you killed him – !'

They slowly stop giggling. Then one of them starts giggling again, and both collapse with laughter but this time with a sense of guilt. They stop.

Pause. They share a handkerchief, wipe their eyes.

Maybe she won't believe it.

MELITTA. She's not stupid.

PAULA. No.

MELITTA. It'll kill her.

PAULA. Yes, it very likely will.

MELITTA. Except she could have left it here. It could be in this room.

They gaze around the room.

PAULA. What was the book you thought I'd moved?

MELITTA. *The Interpretation of Dreams.*

PAULA *stands up.*

PAULA. That seems significant.

Goes to the bookshelf. Removes the book and takes the keys out.

I thought so. Catch.

She throws them across the room. MELITTA *catches them.*

Have a look.

MELITTA *opens the filing cabinet.*

(*Whispers.*) Go on.

MELITTA *opens the top drawer to its fullest extent. The cabinet topples forwards into her arms. She struggles to push it back.* PAULA *runs to help her.*

MRS KLEIN *comes in, dressed for travel as last seen.*

MRS KLEIN. Melitta?

MELITTA. Mother?

MRS KLEIN. Paula, you're a big strong girl, if you could help the taxi fellow with my luggage.

PAULA *goes out.*

So: I'm back.

MELITTA. What happened?

MRS KLEIN. Aren't you pleased to see me? Give your mother a kiss.

They kiss.

Look in your handbag, I've no money, only marks and travellers' cheques.

MELITTA *does.*

It's wonderful you're here, my darling. Stay the night. Your room's the same. I've kept it as it was. Some books are new, some boxes, half a billiard table, as a matter of fact it's packed with rubbish. Stay.

PAULA *comes in with luggage.*

PAULA. One more bag to come. He wants his fare.

MRS KLEIN. I'm not surprised. He's just got married. To a nice Irish girl, he tells me, and they have some minor sexual problems but I think I've helped him. (*To* MELITTA.) How're we doing?

MELITTA. I've got a shilling.

MRS KLEIN. That's no good, the fare is four and ninepence.

MELITTA. Paula's got some money, haven't you, Paula?

MRS KLEIN. Thank you, Paula.

PAULA *crouches and looks round the floor for the money from the pin box.*

PAULA. I'm sorry, it must have rolled.

MRS KLEIN (*to* MELITTA). What's she up to?

PAULA. Got it.

MRS KLEIN. Quite a party you've been having.

PAULA *gives her the two half-crowns.* MRS KLEIN *takes more money off* MELITTA.

Sixpence for the tip, that's five and thruppence. Off you go now.

PAULA *goes.*

MELITTA. Did you get my letter?

MRS KLEIN. Later. What's she doing here?

MELITTA. Working late.

MRS KLEIN. I wish she'd go. She found the keys, I notice. And the whiskey. Make me a cup of tea. I need to make a note of something, personal, not unpleasant. Turn the heating on.

MELITTA *goes out.* MRS KLEIN *loosens her shoes. Takes hat off. Puts a record on. Slow movement, Haydn, Quartet in C major, Op. 54, No. 2.*

* * *

Interlude

Not very long but masks a pause longer than a usual dip in the action. MRS KLEIN *searches her memory for a dream of which she can remember only a fragment. Listens to the music. Some of the dream comes back to her. It astonishes her. She gets her notebook and writes in it. Wipes her eyes, remembers more. Makes more notes. At some point* PAULA *comes in with a suit-case.*

MRS KLEIN. I'm working.

PAULA *puts it down quietly and goes out.*

MELITTA *comes in with a tray untidily laden with tea things.*

End of interlude.

* * *

MELITTA. Paula's sitting in the hall.

MRS KLEIN. At least she's quiet.

MELITTA. Be nice to her.

MRS KLEIN *goes to the door and calls through it.*

MRS KLEIN. Paula, we've got an extra cup. Come in for a moment.

PAULA *does. They all sit.*

Now, who's going to be Mother?

MELITTA. That's your job.

MRS KLEIN. Do it! Paula has an Underground to catch.

MELITTA. She missed it hours ago.

MRS KLEIN. So how's she getting home?

MELITTA. I'm driving her.

MRS KLEIN. You can't, you're sozzled.

MELITTA. I am not!

MRS KLEIN. I'm teasing you, my darling. Pour the tea.

MELITTA *pours tea.*

That's my girl. I've earned my rest. I am exhausted. But euphoric. Something wonderful has happened. Dover Station. In the buffet, where I ate a cheese and pickle sandwich, quite disgusting, first I dozed and then I fell asleep. A wooden bench. A lucky bench because I dreamt on it.

She pauses, takes MELITTA*'s hand.*

I know this tea, it's kitchen tea, it comes from Mrs Pountney's caddy. It's the nicest cup of tea I've ever tasted.

MELITTA. Tell me about the dream.

MRS KLEIN. I saw a mother and son.

She glances at her notebook.

The woman glanced at me in a dismissive way, because I was only a child. A small child. I was struck by the smartness of her black dress and her lace collar. And some childlike instinct told me that the son whose hand she was holding was either about to die or had died already. I didn't feel sad. I felt hostile to them both. Then I woke. I saw the boat-train just about to leave for London so I took it.

MELITTA. What about the boat?

MRS KLEIN. The boat had left.

MELITTA. You missed it?

MRS KLEIN. I decided not to take it.

PAULA. Why the resistance?

MRS KLEIN. Paula, look in the fridge, you'll find some nice salami.

PAULA *goes.*

I didn't like to say while she was here. It struck me just in time that I could not attend the funeral for an obvious reason.

MELITTA. What?

MRS KLEIN. I might have met your father.

MELITTA. And?

MRS KLEIN. He might have propositioned me.

MELITTA *breaks into surprised laughter.*

No good?

MELITTA. No good. Besides, he's married.

MRS KLEIN. Not that *that* would stop him. No, you're right. There's something deeper. Deep resistance. Do me a favour. Don't tell her. How long's she staying?

MELITTA. As long as I do.

PAULA *comes in with salami, plates and a knife.*

MRS KLEIN. Paula, you're staying the night. (*To* MELITTA.) Where's she sleeping?

MELITTA. Sofa.

MRS KLEIN (*to* PAULA). Sofa.

MELITTA (*this is a routine they used to do in the past*). So: this mother.

MRS KLEIN. So, this mother. Mother and son. A dying son.

MELITTA. Or dead.

MRS KLEIN. Who told you dead?

MELITTA. Look at your notes.

MRS KLEIN. No, I believe you. But he wasn't Hans. Because the mother wasn't me. I was a child.

PAULA. What about the dress?

MRS KLEIN. Too much prompting. Find the salami. Dress, a dress, quite right, black dress, lace collar which I –

She touches the lace collar of the black dress she's wearing.

– which I'm wearing at this moment. So: a hint of my unconscious knowledge that it's I who am bereaved. So my denial is weakened. Only slightly. Quite a long way to go. (*Sees the salami.*) You found it, thank you.

Starts cutting it up.

In my childhood, in the summer, we would go on picnics. All the family. And my father would sit on a stump and say to me: 'Melchen, darling, here's a nice thin piece of salami.' And he'd cut it.

She gives a thin piece to PAULA.

And he'd give it to me. Then he'd turn to my older sister, and he'd say: 'And now a nice thick slice of salami for my favourite daughter.'

She gives a thick piece to MELITTA. *Cuts more salami and gives it all to* MELITTA.

Now this, Melitta, was a learned man, a student of the Talmud, what was called a *bocher*, spoke in German, English, Slovak, French he learned from some old chap who fought at the Battle of Waterloo, and yet unthinkingly he stirred up envy between two siblings.

PAULA (*wanting another piece of salami*). Could I – ?

MRS KLEIN. – have a bath, of course.

MELITTA. It won't be hot yet.

MRS KLEIN. True, it will be cool and healthy. (*To* MELITTA.)
  Run the taps.

PAULA. I'd rather –

MRS KLEIN. Fine, you do it yourself.

PAULA. I wonder if you'd mind if –

MRS KLEIN. Bathtime.

  PAULA *goes out, leaving* MRS KLEIN *and* MELITTA
  eating salami.

MELITTA. Did you take my – ?

MRS KLEIN. Have children.

MELITTA. Mother.

MRS KLEIN. I'm broody. I want to be a nice warm bobba. I
  want to smell of cooking oil and make-up. I want enormous
  corseted hips for little boys to throw their arms round.

MELITTA. Did you read my letter?

MRS KLEIN. No.

MELITTA. I guessed you hadn't.

MRS KLEIN. I'm sorry.

MELITTA. If you give it back I'll write you an up-to-date one.

  MRS KLEIN *indicates the filing cabinet.*

MRS KLEIN. Bottom drawer.

  MELITTA *looks for her letter and finds it.*

  The middle drawer contains my dealings with the world. I
  call it my ego drawer. The top drawer is my super-ego
  drawer, it's full of bills and tax reminders, all those harsh
  commands that come from up on high. The bottom drawer is
  dark and filled with menace.

MELITTA. You put my letter in your id drawer!

MRS KLEIN. Yes, who cares. Don't stand there like an idiot,
  darling, sit beside me.

MELITTA. Shouldn't I make the beds up?

MRS KLEIN. They can wait.

MELITTA. She'll need a towel.

MRS KLEIN. She'll find one. No, I locked them up. I locked the soap up. You should have seen me these last few days. You missed some fine old paranoid symptoms. Sit.

MELITTA *does*.

That's better. In a moment, in the fridge, you'll find some nice *Gewürztraminer*. It will go with what we're eating.

MELITTA. Fine.

MRS KLEIN *glances at the letter.*

MRS KLEIN. What's in that letter?

MELITTA. Paula tells me you were hostile towards it.

MRS KLEIN. I thought you were attacking my criminality paper. Quite absurd. I saw the address and – Let me see it.

MELITTA *hands it to her.*

Yes, it was the way you'd underlined the 'Mrs'. *Mrs* Klein. Like you're the learned doctor, I'm the unqualified amateur.

MELITTA. Show me.

MRS KLEIN *gives it to her.*

That's a smudge.

MRS KLEIN *takes it back. Looks.*

MRS KLEIN. So who made it?

MELITTA. The postman probably.

MRS KLEIN *puts glasses on, looks harder.*

MRS KLEIN. There you are, I had a persecutory delusion. I felt my little torch of knowledge being crapped on yet again, you'll pardon me, that's what it feels like when it happens. Though it isn't you I blame, my darling. Glover's the worst.

She slices a piece of salami.

MELITTA. You mean the *wurst*.

MRS KLEIN. Yes, Glover's the *wurst*.

Playfully stabs the salami. Laughs.

Somebody told me Edward Glover took his Easter holiday inside a cloud. Right in one. With his wife and little backward daughter, whom he loves and takes wherever he goes, despite, or possibly because of her condition. So. They went to Scotland. Up a mountain. Right to the top. Set up camp and then the mist descended. So they couldn't leave their tent. But Edward Glover stuck to plan and stayed there for a fortnight, while his wife and daughter begged for mercy. Finally he upped their pegs and down the slope they walked and not a quarter of a mile below are sunny fields and rippling brooks and people in their bathing costumes. The weather was fine, there was a tiny cloud up there, that's all, and in his boring daddy's dogmatism he had spent his holiday inside it.

MELITTA *laughs.*

Perhaps you agree with him less these days?

MELITTA. Rather more.

Pause.

MRS KLEIN. You *will* attack my criminality paper.

MELITTA. Probably. Yes.

MRS KLEIN. In the *Journal*?

MELITTA. Probably in the *Journal*. In the *Journal*.

MRS KLEIN (*suddenly angry*). Why do you do this?

Pause.

What I write, I've learned and proved in twenty years of clinical practice. And you've seen the results.

MELITTA. I have. You're a great clinician. But, Mother, you can't write rubbish and expect me not to say it's rubbish.

MRS KLEIN. No, I don't, because I know you see the so-called rubbish, 'dreck' you called it once, the *poisonous faeces*, aimed at you in person. I can see it, everyone else can see it. It's an embarrassment. Why exhibit your sores in public, darling?

MELITTA. Sores?

MRS KLEIN. Yes, sores, emotional sores. If I fought back you'd see some dreck all right. I could finish your career. Only I won't attack my daughter.

MELITTA (*suddenly angry, shouts*). No, you get your little toadies to attack your daughter.

MRS KLEIN. I don't write papers for my fellow thinkers.

MELITTA. You'll do anything to win. You pack committees, you fiddle agendas, you steal other people's patients.

MRS KLEIN. When did I steal a patient? Whose damn patient?

MELITTA. Mine last month.

MRS KLEIN. He begged for refuge. You confused him. You're a bad clinician.

MELITTA. Why?

MRS KLEIN. You want the truth? Good, fine. You reassure your patients. When they cry, you hug them. And you say their clouds have silver linings and you give them tips on life. What can they learn from that about themselves? All they learn is that you're nice to them, which as a matter of fact you aren't, you're bloody destructive. Take that patient. All his life, like everyone else, he has projected his infant experiences on to the people around him. But it's only now, with me, that he starts to see them. Now, in that powerful, terrifying thing we call the transference. Because, unlike his wife or child or you, I am detached. So he projects those images from his cradle onto an empty screen. You obscured that screen with your emotions. You felt pity. You felt protective. Rubbish. Dreck, dreck, dreck. If you want to be an analyst of any worth you have to trust your patients with the truth. However harsh. They're strong. They'll take it.

MELITTA *gives her her letter.*

What is it?

MELITTA. It's the truth about Hans.

Goes out.

End of Act One.

ACT TWO

Later.

MRS KLEIN, *in silence.* MELITTA*'s letter is there, unopened.*
A bottle of wine. PAULA *comes in quietly and sits somewhere*
out of the way.

MRS KLEIN. Where's Paula?

PAULA. I'm Paula. Melitta's upstairs. She's having a bath.

MRS KLEIN *pours wine for them both.*

MRS KLEIN. I've had two great depressions in my life. One
when I was an angry housewife. One in Berlin when nobody
paid enough attention to me. Now depression number three
is looming. It's like a thick black line just over my field of
vision.

She opens MELITTA*'s letter. Glances at a page.*

Should I read Melitta's letter?

PAULA. Perhaps not now.

MRS KLEIN. Quite right.

She tears it up. Throws the bits of paper in the waste-paper
basket.

Pause.

Deep depression.

Pause.

So. My dream.

PAULA. Your mother and son.

MRS KLEIN. *This* mother and son. And the association runs as
follows. Childhood, picnic, father, sibling envy, Battle of
Waterloo. That's hopeless. Homework.

Thinks.

There is a nasty woman comes to mind who brought her equally nasty son to help my brother with his homework. I was eight years old. It seems to me that mother and son was them.

PAULA. Why dream about them now?

MRS KLEIN. Because I never forgot that evening. It was horrible, frightful. Everyone was upset. My mother was in tears. My brother rushed into his room and slammed the door. He felt utterly humiliated by their offer of help.

PAULA. What did you do?

MRS KLEIN. I sat in the parlour, and I laughed.

She thinks about this.

I'm feeling worse now. As though that thick black line is getting lower.

MELITTA *comes in carrying bedclothes.*

MELITTA. I've come to say goodnight. If we're still talking to each other.

MRS KLEIN. We're still talking.

MELITTA. Did you open it this time?

MRS KLEIN. Yes, I did.

MELITTA. And how do you feel?

MRS KLEIN. I feel severe depression coming on, but I'll survive it.

MELITTA. Good. I mean, that you'll survive it.

MRS KLEIN. I'll survive it.

MELITTA. No hard feelings?

MRS KLEIN. Not on a conscious level.

MELITTA. I was sitting in the Wigmore Hall tonight and thought about it and I –

MRS KLEIN. Let's not talk about it now. All right?

MELITTA. All right.

MRS KLEIN. And so.

MELITTA. And so. Did you really mean to get there?

MRS KLEIN. Where?

MELITTA. To Budapest.

MRS KLEIN. It seems unlikely.

MELITTA. But you would have done. If I'd gone with you. If I'd dragged you.

MRS KLEIN. If you'd dragged me, yes, I might have.

MELITTA (*to* PAULA). We used to live in a flat right under the castle. Big tall shutters. Always dark inside. (*To* MRS KLEIN.) We could have gone to see it. We could have had coffee and cakes together. I could have cheered you up.

MRS KLEIN. That's not your *métier*.

MELITTA (*abruptly to* PAULA). Two sheets. Three blankets. Say if you want an extra pillow. Would you rather sleep upstairs?

PAULA. The couch is fine.

MELITTA. The sofa.

PAULA. What?

MELITTA. The couch comes next week. Or haven't you asked her yet?

MRS KLEIN. If you mean that Paula wants to be my patient, I had guessed as much. She'll ask me in her own good time and I'll consider it then. Goodnight.

MELITTA. Goodnight.

PAULA. Goodnight.

MRS KLEIN (*more kindly*). Melitta.

MELITTA. Yes?

MRS KLEIN. Don't turn the heating off.

MELITTA. I wasn't going to. Night.

She goes.

PAULA. That was tactless of her.

MRS KLEIN. She'll be back.

MELITTA *comes back in.*

MELITTA. What about my letter?

MRS KLEIN. It's the middle of the night, for God's sake. I've been travelling. I'm depressed. I'm in mourning.

MELITTA. So am I.

MRS KLEIN. So what do you want, to bully me about it? Give me time.

MELITTA. We'll talk about it over breakfast.

PAULA. If she doesn't want to read it then she shouldn't have to.

MELITTA. You mean she *hasn't* read it?

MRS KLEIN. Paula, *that* was tactless.

MELITTA. But she said she had. She said…

MRS KLEIN. If I may clarify? I opened it and Paula told me not to read it so I tore it up.

MELITTA. You tore it up?

MRS KLEIN. It was excessive of me. Something is being resisted.

MELITTA. Yes, it is!

MRS KLEIN. But what?

MELITTA. I'll tell you.

MRS KLEIN. Good, you tell me. Well?

PAULA. I'll go upstairs.

MRS KLEIN. I want you here.

MELITTA. Why can't we talk about it just we two?

MRS KLEIN. Because there's no such thing as just we two.
There's always a third. At least a third. The mother. Perhaps
the father, perhaps a rival sibling. Always the room fills up.
Start with two, why not with three? Either way we'll end up
throwing a party. Good, let's start.

MELITTA. Last Friday, Hans was –

MRS KLEIN. In your opinion, Hans's death was not what it
appeared. I read that far.

MELITTA. He left the –

MRS KLEIN. Then my depression deepened, so I stopped.

MELITTA. Mother.

MRS KLEIN. Yes?

MELITTA. Listen.

MRS KLEIN. Go on. Go on.

MELITTA. Last Friday, Hans left the boarding house where he
was staying in Rosenberg.

MRS KLEIN. Not Rosenberg, my dear. You're stuck in the past.
It was Rosenberg when you and he lived there as children.
After the war the name was changed. It's called
Ruzomberok. Which means the same. One moment, please.

She pauses and puts her hand over her eyes.

I sense an inky blackness running from left to right. Well?

MELITTA. He left the boarding house –

MRS KLEIN. You think of it as Rosenberg because the name
evokes a time of primitive content. Before all this. My pres-
ence gave you warmth and comfort.

MELITTA. You were hardly ever there.

MRS KLEIN. I wasn't well. And so the doctor did what doctors
do, prescribed a holiday and then another, then a rest-cure
and they all joined up.

MELITTA *laughs*.

And you were cared for by your bobba. Who was God's own housewife. She was a saint on earth as long as she was not one's mother. That was my little problem and I failed to solve it and I got depressed.

MELITTA. You could have written.

MRS KLEIN. The way I felt I would have depressed you too.

MELITTA. You missed my birthday.

MRS KLEIN. Oh, so now we get to the momentous crisis. I missed your birthday and you're scarred for life.

MELITTA. I am. Not only / because of that, but...

MRS KLEIN. And maybe the cat jumped on your cradle so now you can't drink milk. Melitta, that is popular psychology, it's rubbish, it's for chambermaids. So you had a bad experience, rise above it. Take it to your analyst, she's good, I like her. Where'd we got to? Yes: he left the boarding house and – Let me tell you something. I would walk you to the square. And find a bench. When you were five or six, a difficult age, and Hans was three. I'd buy you ice creams and I'd introduce you to the pigeons. And I'd watch the fountain. And I'd sit and wait to go back home where Mother would have staked her claim to Jewish motherhood by cooking a five-course dinner. And I'd feel despair. That this was it. My life. My waste of life. So I escaped. And don't think you've got cause to feel resentful. You've a doctorship, a fine career and if you choose to throw it all away that's your decision. Now: he travelled to the mountains. How?

MELITTA. He took the bus. He bought a single ticket.

MRS KLEIN. No, that doesn't make sense. To get the special rate you buy two tickets, one to get there, one to come back. Has the system changed?

MELITTA. He wasn't coming back.

MRS KLEIN. I'm confused. Paula, explain.

PAULA. He –

MELITTA. Mother, what do you think I'm trying to tell you?

MRS KLEIN. What?

Pause.

You mean he…

Pause.

And this is how you spring it on me?

MELITTA. Mother –

MRS KLEIN. Let me say, his recent letters gave no cause for worry. He was well and happy. Two weeks ago he wrote to tell me all about a Cossack costume that he'd put together for a party. Boots from somebody at work, the hat from a costume shop. Two whole pages. Quite a tedious letter. It was not the letter of someone who was about to, to kill himself.

MELITTA. He was / wearing…

MRS KLEIN. Wait, wait, wait. How do you know he only bought a single ticket?

MELITTA. The return half wasn't in his pockets.

MRS KLEIN. How do you know?

MELITTA. Aunt Jolan searched them.

MRS KLEIN. How do you know that? Did she telephone you?

MELITTA. I telephoned her.

MRS KLEIN. That says something.

MELITTA. Can I go on?

MRS KLEIN. I'm here, I have no patients waiting.

MELITTA. Only Paula.

MRS KLEIN. Paula's listening. Paula's fine. Continue.

MELITTA. He was wearing ordinary weekday shoes, not climbing boots.

MRS KLEIN. I hear you.

MELITTA. He'd taken nothing to read.

PAULA. This is ridiculous.

MRS KLEIN. Let her go on. She needs it. Well?

MELITTA. He took nothing to eat.

MRS KLEIN. So there's a restaurant in the mountains.

MELITTA. He ate breakfast there. He left a tip. He gave the
waiter all his change. He'd nothing left.

MRS KLEIN. No banknotes?

MELITTA. No.

MRS KLEIN. His wallet?

MELITTA. Empty.

PAULA. Somebody could have robbed the body.

MRS KLEIN. I hadn't visualised him as a... It might be better
if you kept your comments to yourself. (*To* MELITTA.) Go
on.

MELITTA. They found him at the foot of the cliff that looks
back over Ruzomberok.

MRS KLEIN. Ah.

MELITTA. Do you know it?

MRS KLEIN. No, I – No.

She turns away.

MELITTA. It's a beauty spot. Sunday trippers stop to use the
telescope. We went there often, he and I, as children. There's
a riverbed below. We used to stand on the edge when Bobba
wasn't looking. Trying to make our stomachs churn. He
knew it well. He'd seen it a hundred times. So why go back?

PAULA. Why not? A favourite place, why not go back? He
didn't feel like climbing. That's why the shoes were wrong.
No book. Was he a student?

MRS KLEIN. He was a chemist in a paper mill.

MELITTA. Hans never went anywhere on his own without a book. He read all the time. Except when he was fourteen, when you stopped him.

MRS KLEIN. Stopped my son from reading books? That would be unique in central Europe.

MELITTA. Mother, you did.

MRS KLEIN. I don't remember it and I don't believe it.

MELITTA. You told him the books were symptomatic of his hero-worship for his father. So he stopped.

MRS KLEIN. He stopped himself.

MELITTA. You stopped his music lessons.

MRS KLEIN. I did not, he stopped attending them. I went on paying for weeks since nobody told me.

MELITTA. He stopped because you told him that wanting to play the violin was a repressed masturbation fantasy.

MRS KLEIN. It sounds extreme because you've isolated it.

MELITTA. You even stopped him being in love.

MRS KLEIN. This is cheap.

MELITTA. He was in love with a boy at school. You broke them up.

MRS KLEIN. If Hans were truly homosexual I would have accepted it. Although I might not like it. But he isn't. Wasn't.

MELITTA. Then there was that actress, and you said she was a mother-figure with a penis.

MRS KLEIN. Did you see her?

MELITTA. Then that very decent Polish girl. You stopped that too. You said she interfered with the analysis.

MRS KLEIN. She did. That summer we were getting nowhere, then her father was transferred, she left town and we made good progress.

PAULA. Who was 'we'?

MRS KLEIN (*to* MELITTA). So, tell her.

MELITTA. My mother analysed Hans for three hundred and seventy hours from the time he was thirteen to the age of sixteen-and-a-half. She analysed us both. We were her first patients. She wrote us up. I'm Lisa in *The Role of School in Libidinal Development*. Remember? How does it go? 'She has so far (she is now fifteen) shown only an average intelligence.' That was me. That's what she wrote about me.

MRS KLEIN (*to* PAULA). It seemed important to remain detached.

MELITTA. But, Mother.

MRS KLEIN. Yes, I know.

PAULA. She was your daughter.

MRS KLEIN. Yes.

Pause.

MELITTA. I'd lie there trying to think up what to say to her. Trying to think of something so banal, so ordinary that she couldn't interpret it. My history lesson. 'What's history about?' she'd ask me. In her clinical voice. My mother in her clinical voice, imagine. I'd say: 'Oh, history lessons, that's what people did in ancient times, battles and so on.' She'd say: 'What happened in ancient times is you, the infant, seeing your father and me having sexual intercourse. *That's* the battle.' It sounds absurd. It wasn't. That was the worst of it: she's so damn good. I felt that slotting into place, the snap, the 'Yes, that's right.' And I'd be stuck with a horrible truth about myself I couldn't deal with. I wanted to protect her from it, but she wouldn't let me. Kept on sucking it out. My poison. Kept returning it. She used to light her cigarette, her special way, the match pushed forward so the sparks shot into my lap. That was my hatred flying back. It filled the room. The carved brown cabinet stood there waiting for my command to fall and crush her. Or the mat to trip her up. She spilled the ashtray. Muck on the varnished floor. My vengeful shit. All that was good, destroyed. My mother destroyed. My fault. My guilt.

MRS KLEIN. I did good work.

MELITTA. And the results?

MRS KLEIN. You're not so bad. It's Dr Schmideberg I'm not
too fond of.

MELITTA. I'm Dr Schmideberg. Can't you understand?

MRS KLEIN. I'm Melanie Klein.

Pause.

Is there more about Hans?

MELITTA. Yes. Somebody saw him.

MRS KLEIN. When he was on the mountain?

MELITTA. No. Before that.

MRS KLEIN. Who? Who saw him?

MELITTA. The Lutheran pastor in Ruzomberok. Jolan told me.

MRS KLEIN. Well?

MELITTA. He was waiting for a train first thing that morning.
He was on the platform at the station. And he noticed Hans.

MRS KLEIN. The railway station?

MELITTA. Yes. The pastor asked him where he was going.
Hans said, to Budapest. The pastor said, good, we can share
a compartment. Hans refused. He said he wanted to smoke.
He seemed nervous. The pastor said, is something wrong?
Hans said no. But the pastor didn't believe him.

MRS KLEIN. Why was Hans going to Budapest?

MELITTA. To see Aunt Jolan. So he said.

MRS KLEIN. Go on.

MELITTA. He asked the pastor to forgive him.

MRS KLEIN. To forgive him?

Pause.

Is there more?

MELITTA. He said he hoped the pastor wouldn't be shocked by something he might hear about him. He said he was sure that what he was doing was right.

MRS KLEIN. That's all?

MELITTA. That's all.

MRS KLEIN. So he planned to go to Jolan perhaps to find some comfort in her.

MELITTA. But he changed his mind. He never caught the train.

MRS KLEIN. He went to the square and caught the bus to the mountain. Yes, that feels right, I see it.

Pause.

Will it affect the place of burial?

MELITTA. No.

MRS KLEIN. Is there not some kind of religious rule about…? You know what I'm asking.

MELITTA. Nobody knows what happened.

MRS KLEIN. Just us. That's good.

About to pour herself another glass. To MELITTA.

You'll have some now?

Pours a glass. MELITTA *accepts it.*

What none of us cares to ask is why a healthy, reasonably happy young man of twenty-seven should take his own life. Paula, you're too polite to ask. (*To* MELITTA.) You're too defensive. I'm too frightened. No, I'm damn well not.

PAULA. None of us knows / that he really…

MRS KLEIN. Oh, yes, we know.

PAULA. He didn't leave a message.

MRS KLEIN. He did. Though it was probably unconscious. It was meant for me. He chose a place that looks across the valley towards Ruzomberok. Rosenberg. Rose mountain. The breast. Now that's indicative.

PAULA. It isn't your fault.

MRS KLEIN. Don't reassure me. When Hans was an infant, what was the first preoccupation of his ego?

PAULA. The breast.

MRS KLEIN. The breast. The breast on to which the child projects the warmth and goodness that he feels. The good breast. And its opposite. When the child is angry, envious. When his anticipation turns from love for the good-but-yet-to-come, to hatred for the good that seems so miserly with its goodness. This is the breast the infant, in its primitive mind, attacks. Tramples, kicks, annihilates, pinches, mangles, gnaws, tears apart, devours, pierces, poisons with imagined faeces. This is the breast on to which the child *projects* his murderous hatred. So that the breast itself seems hateful. The bad breast. And the prototype for adult fear and dread.

You'll have some more?

Pours wine for PAULA.

No wish to boss you about, my dear, but you'll be very little help to your neurotic patients until you lead them by the hand back to that primitive jungle. Which is wild and strange as only a jungle can be. And *illimitably* rich. You can do it. You've had a child. (*Of* MELITTA.) She has problems in this area, no, she knows my feelings, I can say this.

MELITTA, *unnoticed by her mother, starts to cry.*

It's when the infant recognises you that something new occurs. He starts the greatest struggle in human life. He sees his mother as a person. Whole, complete. Good and bad together. She, whom he's been torturing in his mind, is the one he loves. This is the dawn of guilt. It leads to fathomless depression. It is out of that depression he must climb in order to become a healthy adult. And it's hard. It hurts. To see what we've done to the one we love, it hurts, it hurts. (*To* MELITTA.) Don't drink.

She removes something from MELITTA's *glass with the tip of her finger.*

Piece of cork. It's gone. Now you're in tears. You wanted to hurt the wicked mother. Now you find she's also the good and loving mother. Hurt the one, you hurt them both. Darling, I am one and the same. You cry. That's good. If I could cry like that, I'd be a happy woman.

MELITTA. It isn't true. There are bad mothers. Mothers who are totally bad. That's what you are. We never felt you loved us. You were interested in us, that's all. But we loved you. Hans loved you terribly, terribly. But you could never accept his love for what it was. You always changed it. Made it yours. Everything had to be yours. Whatever we did, whatever we had, whatever we wanted. You'd make us think we didn't like it. Or you'd choose it for us. Anything. A dress in a shop, a train set, my degree.

MRS KLEIN. I chose your husband?

MELITTA. I was compensating.

MRS KLEIN. Quite.

MELITTA. I was neurotically dependent on you.

MRS KLEIN. So you made a break for freedom.

MELITTA. Yes I bloody well did.

MRS KLEIN. What's interesting is that you chose a man my age. A mother-substitute. And what a disaster he turned out to be. A drunk, a fool. You fled from bondage into bondage. And you always will, as long as you are crippled by your unresolved ambivalence towards me. So, resolve it. I can't. Nobody can but you. It's your job. Do it. The alternative is suicide. Either actual, as in Hans's case. Or else, symbolic, which is how you're going at present. And I can't lose any more children. Help me, darling. Forget the Institute. Forget the rows, the meetings. That's for weekdays. Tonight you are in my house. We're mother and daughter. And I'm saying, Melitta, Melchen, dearest, sweetheart, what must we do to have a sensible, adult, mother-and-daughter friendship?

MELITTA. You don't want one.

MRS KLEIN. How am I stopping it? What do you want? Just say and I'll do it. Or don't you trust me?

MELITTA. No.

MRS KLEIN. Good, so now there's something solid we can start with. Set me a challenge. Try me.

MELITTA. I can't think what to say.

MRS KLEIN. No rush. Free associate. Make yourself comfortable.

MELITTA *sits up straight*.

So do it your own way.

MELITTA. I'm driving down to Glyndebourne next week.

MRS KLEIN. I'm listening.

MELITTA. It's *Così*. I got the last two tickets. I was planning to go with Walter. Now you're back, I still intend to go with Walter.

MRS KLEIN. Good, he should enjoy it.

MELITTA. There are six teaspoons in the kitchen drawer, they used to / belong to –

MRS KLEIN. Take them. Paula dear, this must be dull for you, I'm sorry.

MELITTA. I've bought a dinner service. I chose it myself. It's Susie Cooper, polka dots, I know you'll hate it.

MRS KLEIN. This is superficial. When did either of us have our emotional homes in crockery departments? You're resisting something. Tell me.

MELITTA. There's a blanket in the boot of the car. It's mine. I want it.

MRS KLEIN. You say the blanket but it's not the blanket.

MELITTA. I want the car. I want Sunny.

MRS KLEIN. You *have* Sunny.

MELITTA. I have half of Sunny.

MRS KLEIN. But you only paid for half.

MELITTA. I'll buy you out.

MRS KLEIN. Though, as things stand, you have the use of Sunny whenever you ask.

MELITTA. I don't like asking.

MRS KLEIN. So you want him to yourself.

MELITTA. That's right.

MRS KLEIN (*thoughtful*). You think I can't be trusted not to damage your father's penis?

MELITTA. Mother, I promise you, it isn't a penis. It's a 1927 Sunbeam. You say you let me use it. And you nearly always do. But when you can't, I feel irrationally resentful. And I think it would remove a source of tension between us if we did what adults mostly do, have cars of our own.

MRS KLEIN. Good, fine.

MELITTA. I'll write you a cheque.

MRS KLEIN. Not now, not now –

MELITTA *writes a cheque.*

Well, as it suits you.

MELITTA *gives her the cheque.*

MELITTA. Two hundred and thirty-seven pounds ten shillings. That's half the cost less depreciation plus the licence.

MRS KLEIN. Thank you.

MELITTA. As you see, I plan to stay in London.

MRS KLEIN. That will be nice for me.

MELITTA. So you can stop persuading your eminent friends to buttonhole me at the Institute and tell me how much easier I might find things if I practised in New York.

MRS KLEIN. They don't need any persuasion. People worry about you. New York is beautiful, the people are kind, demand is high, the fees are monstrous. I know the money

racket doesn't interest you, but think of Walter. So we hoped
you would consider it. Which you have. You choose to stay
in London. As your mother, I'm delighted. As your colleague, I must warn you, I shall show no mercy. If your
activities are inconsistent with your membership of the
Society, I shall say so, so will others, you'll be forced to
resign. You'll have to become some kind of therapist non-
sense, thumping cushions with your patients. This may
sound harsh, but it's the truth. Let's have things open and
honest between us. As I know you want. Though I believe
there's something else that you're avoiding.

MELITTA. Yes, there is.

MRS KLEIN. So tell me.

MELITTA. I've changed my analyst.

Pause.

I said I –

MRS KLEIN. I heard you.

Pause.

Just as you were getting somewhere. May I say, I think
you're making a big mistake?

MELITTA. It's fine so far.

MRS KLEIN. Of course, it puts me in a strange position.

MELITTA. Me too.

MRS KLEIN. What do I say to get her to take you back?

MELITTA. I'm not going back.

MRS KLEIN. Why not? You've made your gesture.

MELITTA. No.

MRS KLEIN. You're adamant?

MELITTA. Yes.

MRS KLEIN. But to leave your analyst is a…

MELITTA *laughs*.

Is something funny?

MELITTA. Mother, I said I've *changed* my analyst.

MRS KLEIN. So when did you start with your new one?

MELITTA. Three weeks ago.

MRS KLEIN. I see. Of course, I'm disappointed that you never thought to share your problem with me.

MELITTA. We discussed it and I decided not to.

MRS KLEIN. You've rehearsed this conversation.

MELITTA. Yes.

MRS KLEIN. And am I allowed to know who your new analyst *is*?

MELITTA. Edward Glover.

MRS KLEIN *throws her wine at her.*

MRS KLEIN. Drink that.

She grabs scraps of MELITTA*'s letter out of the waste-paper basket.*

Eat these. Eat these. I'll stuff them down your throat. Poisoner. Eat. Eat.

She hits and attacks MELITTA, *rubbing bits of paper into her face and hair.* MELITTA *doesn't resist.* PAULA *pulls her off.* MRS KLEIN *sits, surprised by her actions.* MELITTA *sits.* PAULA *watches. Each of them ends up in a different part of the room from before.*

PAULA (*to* MELITTA). Melitta?

MELITTA. Leave me alone, the pair of you.

MRS KLEIN. Why don't we all sit quietly for a moment. Just we three.

Pause.

I say we three. Though, as a matter of fact, we've quite a crowd collecting. (*To* MELITTA.) If you end up staying with Glover – which I don't advise. But if you do –

MELITTA. Mother.

MRS KLEIN. Listen. If you do. You'll need to watch the counter-transference. Remember his backward daughter. Glover sees you as the brilliant child he's always wanted.

MELITTA. I've thought of that.

MRS KLEIN. Of course, of course. And you should ask your-self who he is.

MELITTA. Glover?

MRS KLEIN. Yes, to you. Just think about it.

MELITTA. I can tell you now. It's been a good three weeks. I see him as the father you betrayed.

MRS KLEIN. That's your perspective. Now I'll tell you why he hates my work. He sees me as the wanton mother casting aside the wonderful father Freud.

MELITTA. He could be right.

PAULA. Melitta is my dead sister.

MRS KLEIN. Well, we all knew that. She's also you: the daughter who fears she isn't loved.

MELITTA. Rubbish.

MRS KLEIN. That speaks volumes.

PAULA (*to* MRS KLEIN). Who was Melitta, when you were trying to drown her in symbolic urine?

MRS KLEIN (*with irony*). Well, I can't imagine.

MELITTA. When she rubbed symbolic faeces in my hair? (*With irony.*) Yes, that's a tough one.

MRS KLEIN. Really, Paula. (*To* MELITTA.) Though, as a matter of fact, I loved my mother. I don't know why I got so nasty about her. All she was, was a typical bossy Eastern-European Jewish momma. There are worse things. I hope.

No response.

I see I can't amuse you.

MELITTA. Who was Hans? To you?

MRS KLEIN. My dream suggests as follows: that my envious triumph when my brother failed in something, was carried over into my feelings towards my son. I loved my son, but I felt a certain degree of malice towards him.

MELITTA. And you wished to harm him?

MRS KLEIN. On some primitive level.

MELITTA. Primitive but effective.

MRS KLEIN. You think I killed him.

MELITTA. He killed you. He killed the you in him.

MRS KLEIN. No, this I can't go along with. He wished to protect the me in him from his sadistic onslaughts. So he killed them, and, in doing so, killed himself. Don't look so sceptical, Melitta. Just because you never protected me from your sadistic onslaughts.

MELITTA. Mother, that's why I'm still alive. Hans died because he couldn't bring himself to hate you.

MRS KLEIN. What about you, you can?

MELITTA. I can. I do.

MRS KLEIN. Although there must be some ambivalence.

MELITTA. No. Not now.

MRS KLEIN. You're saying you hate me, pure and simple. Speak: I'm curious.

MELITTA. Yes.

MRS KLEIN. Although we… sit and talk.

MELITTA. Never again.

She takes a keyring out of her bag. Disentangles a single key.

MRS KLEIN. No, don't do that.

MELITTA (*holds them out*). My key.

MRS KLEIN *looks at her cases.*

MRS KLEIN. I shan't unpack tonight. Paula dear, you'll find a tiny bottle somewhere.

PAULA *looks in a case.*

And I'll need my nightdress.

MELITTA. I hung your blue one over the heater.

MRS KLEIN. That was kind.

MELITTA. That's all it was.

MRS KLEIN. I know.

About to go.

(*To* PAULA.) She was late, you know. Then finally I felt her pushing. In I went. And nothing. Nothing. Off you get, they said, we want the table. No, I cried, he's – He. She was my first-born. I said, I feel him coming. But they heaved me off and I went waddling towards the door. And out she dropped. Just dropped. While I was standing up. And how they laughed. They said – in a nice way – that's how cows have babies. You should call your baby Buttercup. I said: I'll call her little Melanie. Melitta.

She looks at her watch.

Half past five.

PAULA *gives her the little bottle.*

Thank you. My knock-out drops.

PAULA *has also taken out an alarm clock.*

Leave the alarm. I'll sleep in late. Please don't wake me.

PAULA *is about to help her with her coat.*

I can manage.

She goes out.

PAULA. How do you feel?

MELITTA. The same. I'd love a slotting-into-place, or snap or something. Get some sleep. I'll dress and go. Ssh!

PAULA. What?

MELITTA. She hasn't closed her door yet.

They listen. They hear a very slight noise.

PAULA. There.

MELITTA. No, that's the bathroom.

They listen.

When will you start? With her, I mean?

PAULA. She hasn't agreed.

MELITTA. She will.

PAULA. I need her.

MELITTA. Yes.

PAULA. I need her in all kinds of ways.

MELITTA. I know. I always knew it. In my cynical soul. I knew it the moment I saw you working at that desk. I knew.

She holds up a hand to stop PAULA *replying. Listens, then goes out and upstairs.*

PAULA *finds the telephone number* MRS KLEIN *gave her before leaving. Picks up the telephone, dials the operator.*

PAULA. Hello. I want – I'm sorry, I can't speak any louder. I want to make a call to Budapest. 92435. No, personal. Mrs Jolan Vago. V-A – Yes, I'll wait.

Rings off. Picks up a book. MELITTA *comes in, dressed.*

MELITTA. You're up.

PAULA. You left your door key.

MELITTA. I gave it back.

PAULA. She left it here.

MELITTA. She always does. I always take it. But it's different now.

Pause.

Except I always say it's different now. I tell you what. I'll wait till morning. And I'll see how it feels without.

PAULA. Without the key?

MELITTA. Without my mother. If it's fine, or not too bad or can be done without recourse to razors in the bath, I'll –

PAULA. What?

MELITTA. I'll write a book. And leave my husband. Have a child and go to China. In that order. But if not: I'll grovel down from Hampstead Garden Suburb in the morning at about eleven.

PAULA. Take the key.

MELITTA. I have my pride. I think I have my pride.

She picks up the key, then puts it down.

I have my pride. You do keep looking at the phone.

PAULA. I don't. Goodnight.

MELITTA goes out. PAULA starts making up her bed. The telephone rings. She answers quickly.

Mrs Vago? … Hello. I hope I haven't – … I'm calling from London, I'm a friend of Mrs Klein's, I'm – … No, I know she's not. She asked me to ring and tell you that she's very sorry but she won't be coming. … Physically well, but – … Yes, she's very distressed. … I will, Mrs Vago, there was something I wanted to – … I'm a friend of the family. Mrs Vago, there's a very important question I must ask you. It's about Hans. … I know Melitta telephoned you, I – … I think you *do* know. I think there's something you haven't told anyone. And I think you ought to.

The alarm clock goes off. PAULA tries to turn it off while still continuing the conversation.

... It's just an alarm clock, go on. ... I knew it. ... Yes. ... I see, and tell me about the wallet. ... And?

She turns the alarm clock off.

No, Mrs Klein will be relieved. You see, she thought he'd – No, it doesn't matter. ... I'm sure she will, perhaps later on, she's sleeping now. ... Likewise. ... Yes, thank you, yes. God bless you too. Goodbye.

She rings off. Sits and thinks for a moment or two. Turns off the lights. She lies down on the sofa, covers herself with blankets, still thoughtful. Closes her eyes.

Music.

Time passes.

It is some hours later.

Cracks of daylight appear through the curtains.

PAULA *is still asleep.*

MRS KLEIN *comes in. She wears a new dress. She goes quietly and without turning lights on to the filing cabinet.*

PAULA *wakes.*

PAULA. What time is it?

MRS KLEIN. It's not eleven o'clock yet. Go back to sleep.

She rummages in the filing cabinet.

PAULA. I can't.

MRS KLEIN. So maybe it won't disturb you if I draw the curtains.

PAULA *shakes her head.* MRS KLEIN *draws the curtains. Bright spring day outside.*

In my garden I have pigeons, blackbirds, finches, swifts and robins. And I sometimes hear an owl. I find this very reassuring for a London garden. Now, you'll have some coffee?

PAULA. Thank you.

MRS KLEIN. Don't get up.

> MRS KLEIN *goes out.* PAULA *lights a cigarette.* MRS
> KLEIN *comes back in with coffee. Gives it to* PAULA, *goes
> back to her files.*

I'm hunting out my criminality paper. Since I fear it's in the
firing line. Now, where've you got to, naughty fellow. Here.

Finds it.

There's something you could do. If you could stay till
supper. Six o'clock. It's Hans's service then. We'll say a
prayer in Hebrew. You remember any Hebrew?

PAULA. No.

MRS KLEIN. Likewise. Too bad, we'll sit in silence for a
moment. What I must do before is make a difficult call to
Jolan to explain my absence.

PAULA. I've told her.

MRS KLEIN. What?

PAULA. I rang her up last night. I didn't wake you?

MRS KLEIN. No, you didn't but I'm wondering why you took
it upon yourself to trouble her?

PAULA. I did it for you. For you and Hans. I had to. Something
didn't feel right. That letter about his Cossack costume. I
recognised it. I've got a mother and I write to her every
week. She wants two pages or she'll think there's something
wrong. And so she gets them. But I can't exactly tell her the
truth about my life. It's too –

MRS KLEIN. Too what?

PAULA. It's mine. And so I fill it up with trivial things. Just like
he did. He was hiding something. So I moved the material
round and found a different interpretation. And I felt that
snap, that 'yes'. And I rang up Mrs Vago.

MRS KLEIN. So, I'm listening.

PAULA. Hans had fallen in love.

MRS KLEIN. In love?

PAULA. The woman's older – Older than he was.

MRS KLEIN. How much older?

PAULA. In her thirties. She's a singer. Jolan likes her. She lives in Budapest. She has a husband there and children. Two: a boy and a girl.

MRS KLEIN. Surprise me. And?

PAULA. I understood it all. It's simple. Hans was meeting her at the station. They planned to spend the Easter holiday together. He was waiting on the platform and he saw the pastor. He felt nervous. So he lied: he said that he was going to Budapest, to see Aunt Jolan. He warned the pastor there'd be gossip. He asked him to forgive him. But he wasn't ashamed: he knew what he was doing was right. The train came in. They took the bus. She put the tickets in her handbag. He didn't have a book or climbing boots. He didn't need them. They breakfasted together and he left an enormous tip; he wanted to impress her.

MRS KLEIN. Why the mountains?

PAULA. They'd booked a room in the tourist hotel. He left his wallet on the dressing table. The woman took it to Budapest and gave it back to Mrs Vago. She said he'd gone for a walk. While she was getting dressed. Mid-afternoon. She waited. Then she went to find him, and she – That was the first she knew. It seems he'd tried to find a path that isn't there any more. And the ground had fallen away. That's all. That's all.

Pause.

MRS KLEIN. What's interesting is that I feel intense resentment. Not of you, so much, you meant well. But this *woman*, who the hell was she, what's her name?

PAULA. I don't know.

MRS KLEIN. A singer?

PAULA. Yes.

MRS KLEIN. Opera? Cabaret?

PAULA. Mrs Vago didn't tell me.

MRS KLEIN. Had they – ? Yes, she was getting dressed, you
say.

Pause.

I cannot adjust to this. I cannot accept it. (*Angry.*) What the
hell are you trying to tell me, that he died by chance?

Pause. PAULA *shocked and upset.*

He never mentioned her. Not once, not once. Who are her
parents?

PAULA. I didn't ask. Where she comes from, where they met.
It's nothing to do with –

Suddenly angry, shouts.

Don't you see? It's nothing to do with *you*, you stupid
bloody woman. He was free.

MRS KLEIN. No no. The facts remain the same. He…

Pause.

He…

She crumples.

Oh God, I've lost him. I've lost my son.

*She starts to cry. Cries for a long time. After a bit, she holds
her hand out.*

Come.

PAULA *holds her hand. After a bit,* MRS KLEIN *stops
crying.*

Real tears. So my denial is *greatly* weakened. Yes. I'm
starting to recover.

Pause.

I said the facts remained the same. Well, *certain* facts. My
guilt remains. So does my wish to make amends. Now, my
appointment book is somewhere.

She finds it. Opens it.

This is what you want?

PAULA. It is.

MRS KLEIN. Because you must be sure.

PAULA. I'm sure.

MRS KLEIN *looks through her appointment book.*

MRS KLEIN. Where are we?

Stops looking.

Tears, you know, are very much equated with excreta in the unconscious mind. Through tears the mourner casts bad objects into the outside world. You know my fees?

PAULA. I do.

MRS KLEIN. They're what's expected. You must decide to place that value on my time. And yours.

PAULA. I'll manage.

MRS KLEIN. I can offer you Mondays, Wednesdays, Fridays, Saturdays. At eleven a.m. Now, must I put these in my book, you tell me?

PAULA. Eleven o'clock is fine.

MRS KLEIN *writes in her book.*

In fact we're late.

MRS KLEIN. I beg your pardon?

PAULA. It's Saturday now. And look at the clock. We've lost five minutes.

MRS KLEIN. My consulting room is locked. And there's the stairs.

PAULA. Let's stay down here.

MRS KLEIN. It's all too much. I'm utterly exhausted, not this morning. No.

PAULA. Please, Mrs Klein.

MRS KLEIN looks penetratingly at her.

MRS KLEIN. I see. Very well. But from Monday we must be more formal.

PAULA lies on the sofa, pulls a blanket over her feet. MRS KLEIN moves a chair into position.

And not the coffee, please.

She removes the cup.

Pause. MRS KLEIN *sits.*

Whenever you want.

She waits with a singular expression of alertness: her professional manner. Different from the way she's looked at any previous point in the play.

Pause.

PAULA. I'm worried about the doorbell.

MRS KLEIN. You worry that if it rings I might abandon you.

PAULA. I know you won't. You told me yesterday. You said the world must wait.

Pause.

I know this isn't helpful, but I can't help thinking as an analyst. You feel guilty about your children.

MRS KLEIN. Mm-hm.

PAULA. You see the harm you've done to them.

MRS KLEIN. Go on.

PAULA. You want to pay them reparation. But for one of them it's too late.

MRS KLEIN. Mm-hm.

PAULA. You want to pay Melitta reparation.

Pause.

You're doing so now.

Pause.

I terribly want you to reply to that.

MRS KLEIN. You were afraid I'd left you.

PAULA. No. I felt content.

MRS KLEIN. You felt –

The doorbell rings. MRS KLEIN *does not react to it.*

You feel perhaps that you've replaced Melitta as my daughter.

Doorbell.

PAULA. I have.

Doorbell.

MRS KLEIN. Mm-hm.

PAULA. I feel –

MRS KLEIN. I'm listening.

Doorbell.

The End.